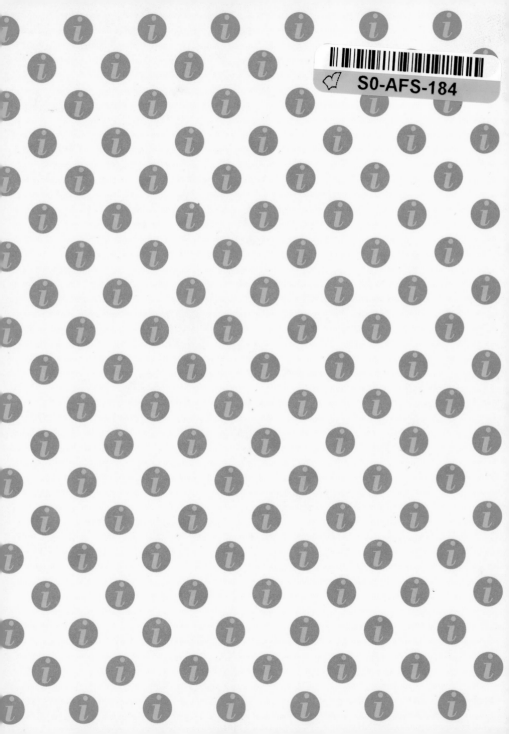

ROSES

The new compact study guide and identifier

IDENTIFYING

i

ROSES

The new compact study guide and identifier

John Mattock

CHARTWELL
BOOKS, INC.

A QUINTET BOOK

Published by Chartwell Books
A Division of Book Sales, Inc.
110 Enterprise Avenue
Secaucus, New Jersey 07094

This edition produced for sale
in the U.S.A., its territories
and dependencies only.

ISBN 0-7858-0052-2

This book was designed and produced by
Quintet Publishing Limited
6 Blundell Street
London N7 9BH

Creative Director: Richard Dewing
Designer: Isobel Gillan
Project Editor: Helen Denholm
Editor: Frederika Stradling

Picture credits t = top, m = middle, b = bottom

All the pictures in this book were taken by the author
except the following:

James Cocker & Sons, Aberdeen, Scotland 55b; Dickson's
Nurseries, Newtownards, Northern Ireland 58b;
E. T. Archive 7t; Fryer's Nurseries, Knutsford, England 39t;
R. Harkness & Co., Hitchin, England 49t, 54t, 54b; Jackson
& Perkins, Oregon, USA 32t, 33t, 36t, 36b, 37t, 38t, 40b,
41b, 42t & b, 43t & b, 45b, 46t, 48m, 50t, 51t, 58t, 59t,
62b, 64m, 68b, 75t; W. Kordes Sohne, Sparrieshoop,
Germany 36m; Sean McCann 56b, 57m, 59b; National
Gallery 8; Oxford Scientific Films 12, 13; Harry Smith
9t & b, 14; F. C. Whitchell 37b, 38b, 40t, 45t, 49b, 51m,
52b, 71b, 72b, 73b, 77b.

John Mattock would like to acknowledge the constructive
advice of Sean McCann.

Typeset in Great Britain by
Central Southern Typesetters, Eastbourne
Manufactured in Singapore by Eray Scan Pte. Ltd
Printed in Singapore by Star Standard Industries Pte. Ltd

CONTENTS

INTRODUCTION 6

History 7

Buying Roses 9

Growing Conditions 9

Planting 10

Maintenance 10

Pruning 11

Pests and Diseases 12

Roses for Special Situations 13

How to Use This Book 14

ROSE IDENTIFIER

Wild Roses 18

Old Garden Roses 22

Modern Shrub Roses 31

Hybrid Tea Roses 35

Floribundas 44

Patio and Miniature Roses 53

Ground-cover and Landscape Roses 61

Climbers and Ramblers 67

Tree Roses 76

Index 80

$\mathcal{I}$NTRODUCTION

A beautiful yellow Floribunda, "Arthur Bell".

*R*osa is the most popular genus of garden plant in the world. In any one selling season between 3,000 and 4,000 cultivars of garden rose are offered to the public. While many older varieties and cultivars fall out of favour, improved lines of breeding and greater disease resistance mean that the number is constantly being added to. A typical mail order catalogue carries about 100 to 140. This handbook describes over 100 cultivars which are currently available and illustrates the development of the rose from its origin as a wild plant, still to be found in many temperate countries of the Northern Hemisphere.

Such is the sophistication of the modern hybrid that it can be grown as an ornamental contribution to the greening of the planet, as a garden plant tolerant of many different soils and climates, and as a high production plant for cut-flower nurseries. This last is big business, as the rose is highly regarded as a token of esteem.

The colour range is very wide and new shades, together with new plant forms, are constantly being introduced.

There are many clubs and societies which provide expert guidance for the new rose gardener, offering practical advice on all aspects of rose growing. All are very helpful and publish a great deal of useful information.

Although most countries boast a rose fraternity, the leading societies are:

The American Rose Society PO Box 30,000, Shreveport, LA 71130, USA

The Royal National Rose Society Chiswell Green, St Albans, Herts AL2 3NR, UK

Verein Deutscher Rosenfruende Waldstrasse 14, 7570 Baden Baden, Germany

HISTORY

The history of the rose offers a glimpse into the history of civilization. The first gardens, in Greek and Roman times, were collections of plants for medicinal purposes. The rose played an important rôle for early herbalists, but was soon used as an ornamental plant to enhance Mediterranean gardens, 2,000–3,000 years ago. The Persians and Egyptians used the rose as a symbol of sophistication, and scattering rose petals was highly fashionable on many social occasions.

The medieval period saw a reversal in

A botanical drawing showing the beauty of this Moss rose, Rosa centifolia muscosa.

An illustration of a medieval garden from the fifteenth-century La Roman de la Rose. *Roses feature in the floral border.*

the fortunes of the rose, as it was associated with the decadence of the Roman Empire. It was grown almost solely (but extensively) for medicinal use. The Renaissance brought about renewed interest in the genus, which was further popularized by painters and poets.

Until the nineteenth century, the roses grown in the West were what we now think of as the old-fashioned kinds: Albas, Damasks, Gallicas and Centifolias. When new varieties or forms appeared it was by chance: occasionally a species produced 'sports', offshoots different in flower colour or form from the parent, which were propagated by cuttings. All these roses had one characteristic in common: they only flowered for a brief period, in late spring and early summer.

The arrival in Europe of the China rose in the nineteenth century was a revelation: *Rosa chinensis* var. *semperflorens* was a perpetual rose (a "remontant"), flowering not once but repeatedly, all summer long. The introduction of this rose into Western Europe, and its subsequent hybridization, heralded the development of the modern rose.

In both the UK and France a few dedicated nurserymen began breeding work, involving hours of painstaking cross-pollination by hand, to combine the repeat flowering of the China rose with the vigour of other species. The result was the first Hybrid Perpetual, "Rose du Roi", in 1816. This red rose was both robust and repeat flowering.

Crossing *Rosa gigantea* with *Rosa chinensis* produced *Rosa x odorata,* the refined Tea Rose with the high-pointed centre and slender buds that are familiar in the Hybrid Tea. Finally, in 1867 Guillot in France crossed a Tea Rose with a Hybrid Perpetual and produced the pale pink "La France", the first Hybrid Tea, although it was not actually recognized as a new type of rose for some years. This combined the vigour of a Hybrid Perpetual with the elegance of a Tea Rose.

Also important in the evolution of the rose was the discovery of the Bourbon rose in the early nineteenth century. A cross between the China and the Damask roses, it was also perpetual. *Rosa foetida persiana,* a double yellow rose, is signifi-

The right wing of the Wilton Diptych, c.1395. Double roses can be seen on the ground.

cant because it is the source of yellow and orange shades in roses.

The rose's subsequent evolution, from the heavy, opulent blooms of the Victorian era to the refined, elegant modern flowers, is a remarkable achievement, which has also been accomplished in a very short time. The ability to flower over very long periods was improved by the introduction, in about 1900, of bright yellows and gaudy bicolours, and the astonishingly bright vermillions which appeared in 1950–60.

BUYING ROSES

The garden rose is now produced in vast numbers in many countries and a visit to the rose fields is an annual expedition for many people. Here the gardener can see the newest varieties, together with old favourites.

Most plants can be chosen through very well-illustrated catalogues and delivered by mail order in the autumn and early spring. Alternatively, you can visit garden centres during the winter, early spring and summer.

Plants delivered by mail order are called "bare root" and are usually planted during the winter months. Alternatively,

Floribundas are cluster-flowered roses and are extremely popular, providing a display of colour that is second to none.

for many gardeners there are great advantages to buying containerized plants, that is, plants in plastic pots or in sleeves, in the spring and summer. The plants avoid the demands of the harsh winter while the gardener can plant when the weather is milder. Many gardeners, particularly of the older generation, still prefer to plant in the autumn with bare-root plants, but there is little to be gained from this. There is a risk of damage to the plant from severe frost and wind.

Miniature roses are a good choice for containers and can also be used for edging and rock gardens.

GROWING CONDITIONS

Roses are extremely tolerant plants and grow in a variety of soils and situations. They are at their most productive in deep fertile soils with an abundance of loam, clay and sand. They do not like very limey or chalky soils (alkaline), and are difficult to grow in those conditions. Similarly, they dislike very acid soils, the sort where rhododendrons and azaleas abound. Roses will not be very productive in badly drained soils, although they will stand occasional seasonal flooding.

As temperate plants they really enjoy a cold, but not harsh, winter with a soft spring and a pleasant summer. Intense heat is anathema and very dry conditions make it impossible to grow quality stock.

Windy situations can be discouraging but usually more to the gardener than the plant. However, roses will not thrive in a persistent draught – the kind of situation created by the over-protective horticulturist with a proliferation of hedges or narrow gaps due to bad building schemes.

Roses are naturally hardy plants but will need some frost protection if planted in zone 4 or below (see page 15).

PLANTING

Roses can be planted at most times of the year, depending on weather conditions and the way in which the new plant arrives at the gardener. Bare-root plants are usually planted between November and March; if the ground is frozen or waterlogged, wait for better weather. Containerized plants can be planted during the summer as well, as long as they are very well watered.

Whatever the season, always prepare the soil thoroughly by digging to a good depth and working in a well-composted organic manure to raise the natural fertility. This should be done well before planting, so that the soil has time to consolidate.

If you are planting a quantity of rose bushes it is a good idea to mark the precise position of each bush. This forward planning will save a lot of time. Most bush roses, whether Hybrid Teas or Floribundas, will fill a bed well if planted some 2ft (60cm) apart. Climbers and ramblers on walls will make a good show of colour planted 8–10ft (2.4–3m) apart.

Prepare a planting mixture consisting of a friable material such as peat, or peat substitute, mixed with bone meal (approximately a bucketful of damp peat to a handful of bone meal). As you plant the bushes, add the planting mixture around the roots to encourage a good root system. Never let the roots of new rose plants dry out; soaking in water before planting will help. Never handle new plants while they are frozen.

MAINTENANCE

During the course of the growing season an established bush rose requires the minimum of maintenance. However, there are certain elementary rules.

The most important is seasonal feeding. Use a *rose* fertilizer, easily obtainable from garden shops. Never apply a general garden feed as this is usually too high in nitrogen and will encourage disease.

Apply this rose feed twice a year. Make the first application early in the spring; immediately after pruning using the proportions recommended by the supplier. Repeat in early summer, to encourage fresh growth to produce an autumn flush of blooms. Never apply this second feed after mid-summer, as the subsequent growth will be too late to produce seasoned wood and will make the plant susceptible to frost damage.

Most rose bushes will need dead-heading immediately after flowering. This simple operation will encourage new growth and is best done by removing the old flowering head and about 9in (23cm) of growth.

Because a rose is grown on a root-stock, wild roses may appear around the base of the plant. These must be removed as they appear and can be identified by the emergence of very pale leaves.

PRUNING

Pruning is the most important exercise in the proper cultivation of the rose. This is the removal of dead and surplus wood to encourage rapid regrowth and the production of good flowering wood.

Bush roses (Hybrid Teas and Flori-bundas) need cutting down by about two-thirds in early spring. Using a very sharp pair of secateurs, first remove any dead or decaying wood completely and then prune back the rest, cutting the stems at a sloping angle to produce a clean cut. As in all garden operations, be sure to remove all detritus and prunings. Never allow rubbish to accumulate.

Climbing and rambling roses need heavy dead-heading, removing the old flowering shoots to within 1in (2.5cm) of the main climbing stems. Preserve all young climbing growth and carefully tie it in as it is produced. Most modern climbers can produce blooms in the autumn, so it is best to prune lightly.

Miniature and patio roses must be pruned by exactly the same method as bush roses, but obviously to a greater degree. By their very nature they appear to accumulate a large amount of thin, scrubby wood which must be cut out.

Correct pruning cut.   *Pruning too close to the bud.*   *Pruning too far from the bud.*

When pruning, cut out dead wood and weak stems.

Pruning a newly-planted hybrid tea.

Shrub roses need little more than light dead-heading and shaping. As they age you may need to cut out the occasional large old stem completely, during the winter months. Never attempt to cut the fabric of a rose when it is frozen.

PESTS AND DISEASES

The modern rose is a relatively healthy plant and needs little in the way of disease protection. However, certain elementary precautions must be taken to give a rose a reasonable degree of resistance. A balanced feeding programme is essential, but you must remember that the rose needs a larger proportion of potash than most other garden plants; therefore it is essential to use a *rose* fertilizer, which has the necessary constituents. Eliminate any dead or decaying material when pruning.

The disease black spot may appear from mid-season onwards, in the form of black circles on the leaf surface. The leaves

eventually fall. Mildew appears as a grey mould on the leaves and rust is first observed as small red spots on the underside of leaves in late summer and autumn. All three fungal diseases can be controlled by a good spray with a systemic fungicide, applied immediately after spring pruning and again in mid- and late summer.

Greenfly should be removed by the use of an aphicide.

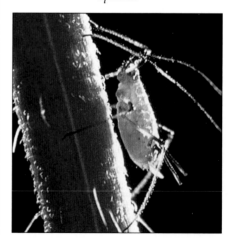

Mildew can be controlled by spraying with a fungicide.

Greenfly (aphids) often appear on young rose foliage in the late spring and must be controlled by the application of a systemic aphicide when first observed. A whole host of beetles and caterpillars occasionally regard the foliage of roses as rather special food. These are easily controlled with a comprehensive spray.

ROSES FOR
SPECIAL SITUATIONS

Planning and planting a rose garden is an enjoyable exercise. For the best results, however, you need to take care choosing the right cultivars and varieties for particular situations.

Modern Hybrid Teas and many Floribundas have most impact planted in conventional rose beds. The most dramatic effects can be obtained by grouping them in blocks of colour. Very large areas will need a lift by adding the occasional pillar rose, tall shrub or tree rose.

Mixed borders of herbaceous plants and shrubs can be enhanced by planting groups of the more vigorous Floribundas and many of the shrub roses. They can give colour when many other plants are past their prime, planted in groups of five or seven about 2–3ft (60–90cm) apart.

Climbing roses are the most suitable for covering walls. Ramblers, which have a more relaxed growth habit, are ideal for pergolas and arches, and for growing through trees. They are very useful for disguising ugly features such as tree trunks or fences. Some climbers will grow on north or sunless walls, but as a general rule most roses benefit from receiving the maximum amount of sun, particularly in the early spring and summer.

HOW TO USE THIS BOOK

This book is laid out so as to provide a concise and clear guide to identifying roses. The identifier section has detailed entries on over one hundred popular roses, ranging from the very old to the very new, each one accompanied by a picture of the rose. Arranged alphabetically in their relevant groups, the entries give brief descriptions of the roses, as well as the breeder, parentage, awards and synonyms. If the breeder and paren-

tage are unknown or inapplicable, as with wild roses, many old garden roses and some climbers, the origin is given instead. In these cases there are no awards. For old garden roses, the type of rose is also given but not awards. The symbols below, which accompany each entry, provide vital information on plant height, flower size, number of petals, frost resistance, flowering and disease resistance.

These roses have been planted in a raised bed to good effect.

HEIGHT

Plant height is relative to climate and geographical location, so it is not possible to quote specific measurements. However, as a general rule, a bush rose can be described as short if it is normally under 2ft (60cm), medium if up to 4ft (1.2m) and tall if up to 6ft (1.8m). A medium shrub is about 3–4ft (90cm–1.2m) and a tall variety 5ft (1.5m) or over.

Tall   Medium   Short

FLOWER SIZE

This is calculated simply on the average diameter of the bloom. A small bloom is about 1.25in (3cm) across, a medium bloom about 4in (10cm) and a large bloom 6in (15cm).

Large   Medium   Small

NUMBER OF PETALS

The number of petals bears no relation to the size of the bloom. Some very small blooms may have dozens of petals, large blooms may only have five or ten petals. The number will depend on whether the bloom is single (less than 8 petals), semi-double (8–20 petals) or double (more than 20 petals).

Single   Semi-Double   Double

FROST RESISTANCE

Most garden roses are frost resistant to about 14°F (−10°C) but will need some protection if these temperatures persist for any length of time. In areas where low temperatures prevail, good catalogues publish plant temperature zones with advice on tolerance to both heat and cold. As a rough guide, zones 3–10 in the chart below, which shows average minimum temperatures, will grow good roses.

Zone 1   Below −50°F (−45°C)
Zone 2   −50 to −40°F (−45 to −40°C)
Zone 3   −40 to −30°F (−40 to −35°C)
Zone 4   −30 to −20°F (−35 to −29°C)
Zone 5   −20 to −10°F (−29 to −23°C)
Zone 6   −10 to 0°F (−23 to −18°C)
Zone 7   0 to 10°F (−18 to −12°C)
Zone 8   10 to 20°F (−12 to −7°C)
Zone 9   20 to 30°F (−7 to −1°C)
Zone 10   30 to 40°F (−1 to 4°C)

FLOWERING

Some of the older shrub roses and most rose species are only summer flowering. Most modern varieties are recurrent (remontant).

Summer   Recurrent

DISEASE RESISTANCE

Resistance to disease depends on the quality of cultivation and the presence of susceptible host plants in the immediate vicinity. Nevertheless, most newer cultivars have a good health record.

Good   Ordinary   Bad

ℛOSE ℐDENTIFIER

WILD ROSES

The wild rose with which we are familiar in the countryside is but one of some 150 species of the genus *Rosa* which can be discovered growing in temperate zones. A peculiarity is that they are only indigenous to the Northern Hemisphere. They vary in stature from tiny roses about 6in (15cm) tall found on barren coasts to enormous plants some 60ft (18m) high in China. Some of them can contribute enormously to the garden, with their distinctive foliage, flowers and, in many cases, splendid display of hips. Most are very hardy. They must be allowed to grow naturally and never pruned or dead-headed. They generally love full sunlight and light, sandy soils.

ROSA FARRERI PERSETOSA ▶

The fern-like foliage of this rose adds to its charm. A semi-sprawling, graceful plant about 5ft (1.5m) tall, the very small, salmon-pink flowers are produced early in the season, with an autumn display of bright red hips. This is a hardy shrub which has the smallest rose flowers in the garden.

Origin   Discovered in China in 1914
Synonyms   The Threepenny Bit Rose

ROSA GLAUCA ▼

A wild rose from Europe which can be propagated easily from seed, this astonishing plant makes a great contribution to the garden with its very deep purple foliage. It has insignificant pink flowers but the rich harvest of small, brilliant crimson hips is a sight never to be forgotten. The fabric of the plant is also a brilliant purple, which garden designers are using with ever-increasing enthusiasm. A healthy plant, it will grow anywhere to about 6–8ft (1.8–2.4m).

Origin   Native to Europe
Synonyms   *Rosa rubrifolia*

ROSA HUGONIS ▼

A very vigorous plant, this is one of the earliest roses to flower. The long stems, which can be 10ft (3m) tall, are clothed in single, primrose-yellow blooms in the late spring with a scattering of small, dark red hips in the autumn. The fern-like foliage is borne on bronze stems. A mature shrub will add grace to the garden.

Origin   Collected in China in 1899
Synonyms   Golden Rose of China

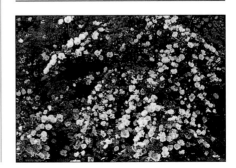

ROSA LONGICUSPIS ▶

This rose has a rambling habit and its rate of growth is very prodigious. Collected originally in north-east India, it grows easily from seed. The milky white flowers with yellow stamens are borne in big clusters in the middle of the summer. The shiny, dark green, leathery leaves are semi-evergreen.

Origin   Discovered in north-east India in 1915

Synonyms   None but can sometimes be mistaken for *Rosa mulliganii*

◀ ROSA MOYESII GERANIUM

Rosa moyesii is probably the most widely grown of all the wild roses. The display of large, flask-shaped hips in autumn is legendary. The type is characterized by a stunning show of bright metallic-red single blooms in mid-summer. Because of its great fecundity of seed it has been planted widely, giving many variations in vigour and colour. The cultivar "Geranium" is by far the best garden form. There is a good pink form, "Sealing Wax".

Origin   Collected in China in 1890 and introduced to Europe in 1894

Synonyms   None

ROSA SERICEA PTERACANTHA ▶

This is a superb shrub, with the unique feature of enormous, translucent thorns. The small pale flowers, produced in early summer, are insignificant but the plant can sometimes produce a small showing of dark hips. The true glory of this rose is the beautiful colour of the young growths. It is best planted to take advantage of the sun shining through the young foliage in early morning or late evening. A vigorous plant, it grows about 9ft (2.7m) tall.

Origin   Discovered in China early in the nineteenth century but not introduced as a garden plant until 1890

Synonyms   *Rosa omiensis pteracantha*

ROSA XANTHINA VAR. SPONTANEA CANARY BIRD ▶

A very popular and widely grown species rose which is prominent in many gardens in early summer, this has rich canary-yellow single flowers covering the length of the stems. The fern-like foliage is an added attraction. In warm gardens it will produce a show of blooms through the summer and autumn. On some acid soils it may suffer from die-back but this is not fatal.

Origin   Introduced from China in 1908
Synonyms   None

OLD GARDEN ROSES

Cultivated garden roses developed from the wild in a relatively
short time and by the fourteenth century there were several easily
identifiable types. Alba roses, mostly white and pink flowers, were
common in the fifteenth century and include the White Rose of
York. Damask roses were popular in the Near East and spread
along the caravan routes. Gallica roses are the origin of the Red
Rose of Lancaster. The Centifolia or Provence rose was the rose of
the old Dutch masters. Its mutation produced the Moss roses.
The introduction of the China roses (see history) gave rise to the
Bourbons, the Portlands and the Hybrid Perpetuals. Another group
from the East, the Rugosas, completes this list. Thus the gardener
can grow a living history of the rose.

BLANC DOUBLE DE COUBERT

This is one of the Rugosa roses developed from an ancient species, *Rosa rugosa*, discovered in Japan. Rugosa roses have strong, leathery foliage and many varieties have wonderful scent and a profusion of large globular hips. This cultivar carries large white flowers with a tremendous scent.

Type Rugosa
Breeder Cochet-Cochet, France 1892
Parentage *Rosa rugosa* x "Sombreuil"
Synonyms None

CHARLES DE MILLS

This amazing variety produces some of the most beautiful blooms in all the Gallicas. The flowers develop to form a wonderful pattern of quartered petals in a mixture of purple and ruby. The stems are long, with deep-green foliage, making this a good cut flower.

Type Gallica
Origin Reputedly discovered before the end of the eighteenth century
Parentage Unknown
Synonyms None

CARDINAL DE RICHELIEU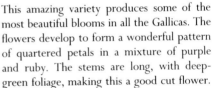

One of the shorter Gallicas, this rose has small clusters of velvety purple blooms which are borne very freely in mid-summer. The thin, lax growth has dark green stems which are practically thornless. The plant should be allowed to grow naturally. It requires very little cutting back and responds well to plenty of nutrients.

Type Gallica
Breeder Laffay, France 1840
Parentage Unknown
Synonyms None

COMMON MOSS

The Moss roses appeared in European gardens by about 1600. They quickly became very popular and proliferated in a short period of time, with some 200 varieties listed. Sadly, these numbers are now depleted. "Common Moss" produces a profusion of very double pink flowers with a lovely perfume in mid-summer. There is a similar white form, "White Moss".

Type	Moss
Origin	Introduced about 1700
Synonyms	"Old Pink Moss", "Miller's Moss", "Communis", *Rosa x centifolia* "Muscosa"

FRU DAGMAR HASTRUP

A single, silvery pink, scented Rugosa rose, this is constantly in flower yet yields typical large globular hips in the autumn. The plant is relatively short but makes a high quality hedge about 4ft (1.2m) tall, requiring little maintenance and virtually disease free.

Type	Rugosa
Breeder	Hastrup, Germany 1914
Parentage	Unknown
Synonyms	"Frau Dagmar Hartopp"

FERDINAND PICHARD ▶

Although a very recent introduction, this is a true replica of many Hybrid Perpetuals popular about 100 years ago. The large, globular flowers are pink, heavily laced and streaked with crimson. With its pleasing fragrance and rich green foliage, it is often described as the finest striped rose in cultivation today.

Type	Hybrid Perpetual
Breeder	Tanne, France 1921
Parentage	Unknown
Synonyms	None

◀ GREAT MAIDEN'S BLUSH

This is generally accepted as the best of the Albas. An upright plant with typical grey-green foliage, it bears clusters of fragrant, double ivory-coral flowers in mid-summer which are very good for cutting. There are many synonyms with beautiful descriptive names.

Type	Alba
Origin	Probably introduced in about 1400
Synonyms	"Cuisse de Nymphe Emue", "Incarnata"

LA REINE VICTORIA ▶

A typical Bourbon, the large, rich lilac-pink globular flowers of this rose were often copied on Victorian embroidery. The long stems are slightly lax in growth but make good material for flower arranging. In common with most of this category of rose, it has a rich fragrance but needs good fertile soil and protection from black spot.

Type	Bourbon
Breeder	Schwartz, France 1872
Parentage	Unknown
Synonyms	None, but it has a pale pink sport, "Mme Pierre Oger", which occasionally reverts to type

MME ISAAC PEREIRE

A large straggling Bourbon, this rose will make a small climber if trained against a wall. The very large rose-pink blooms have a heavy scent – it is probably the most fragrant rose to grace the garden today. The early blooms occasionally have a green eye but this is not a serious problem.

Type	Bourbon				
Breeder	Garçon, France 1882				
Parentage	Unknown				
Synonyms	None				

MME PLANTIER

Apart from the flower colour, this plant is not typical of the true Albas. A well-established plant will spread to 6–8ft (1.8–2.4m) or alternatively grow to a moderate height as a climber. It has lax stems and pale green foliage, and produces flattish flowers of pale cream in clusters. It requires little maintenance apart from cutting out very old wood.

Type	Alba
Breeder	Plantier, France 1835
Parentage	Unknown
Synonyms	None

◀ PAUL NEYRON

The tremendous size of the rich pink blooms are complemented by their delicate sweet perfume. These gigantic blooms are produced on an upright bush clothed with handsome, matt, dark green foliage. It requires a good, deep, fertile soil and plenty of sun. This rose is typical of the Hybrid Perpetuals of the late Victorian and Edwardian eras.

Type	Hybrid Perpetual
Breeder	Levet, France 1869
Parentage	"Victor Verdier" x "Anne de Diesbach"
Synonyms	None

   4-9

PENELOPE ▶

"Penelope" is one of a whole family of shrub roses called Hybrid Musks bred by a parson, the Reverend J. Pemberton, who was also an amateur rose breeder. This range of shrubs has a slightly spreading habit and produces clusters of semi-double blooms. "Penelope" is creamy pink with a pleasant scent. There are similar varieties in a pastel range of colours, including "Buff Beauty" (buff yellow), "Cornelia" (apricot pink) and "Prosperity" (white).

Type	Hybrid Musk
Breeder	Pemberton, UK 1924
Parentage	"Ophelia" x "Trier"
Synonyms	None

    4-10

PINK GROOTENDORST ▶

A continuous flowering Rugosa, "Pink Grootendorst" has clusters of small pink flowers reminiscent of country pinks. The medium-sized plant is highly productive throughout the summer. There is a red form, "F. J. Grootendorst", to which this variety will occasionally revert, but it is not as attractive.

Type	Rugosa
Breeder	Grootendorst, Holland 1925
Parentage	*Rosa rugosa rubra* x "Norbert Levavasseur"
Synonyms	None

REINE DES VIOLETTES ▼

A remarkable Hybrid Perpetual, this upright growing plant has almost thornless stems which support fabulous blooms of velvety violet with a lovely perfume. The medium-sized flowers have an intricate design of quartered and ruched petals, and are good for flower arranging.

Type	Hybrid Perpetual
Breeder	Millet-Malet, France 1860
Parentage	Seedling of "Pius IX"
Synonyms	"Queen of Violets"

ROSA MUNDI ▼

Probably the oldest Gallica in cultivation, this is known to have existed before 1200. The relatively short plants, about 4ft (1.2m) tall, produce an abundance of open, medium-sized flowers in a mixture of light crimson and white stripes, in early summer. The foliage is prone to mildew after flowering but this has not quelled its popularity.

Type	Gallica
Origin	Introduced before 1200
Synonyms	*Rosa gallica versicolor*

ROSA RUGOSA ALBA ▶

An extremely satisfactory hedging plant, *Rosa rugosa alba* produces red, globular hips as large as small tomatoes. The open, pure white, single blooms have a good fragrance. The disease-proof foliage, luxuriant and dark green, is a perfect foil. A handsome shrub about 5ft (1.5m) tall, it requires little maintenance and no pruning.

Rosa rugosa rubra is identical as to growth and hips but has purple-red flowers.

Type Rugosa
Origin Introduced from Japan in the nineteenth century
Synonyms None

ROSERAIE DE L'HAY ▶

An extremely popular Rugosa, this will produce a fine shrub about 6ft (1.8m) tall. The disease-proof, strong, leathery foliage and thorny stems bear large, semi-double royal purple flowers with a strong scent. Rarely out of flower from late spring to early autumn, it sadly lacks the crop of hips so characteristic of other Rugosa roses.

Type Rugosa
Breeder Cochet-Cochet, France 1901
Parentage Probably a sport from an unknown Rugosa seedling
Synonyms None

◀ WILLIAM LOBB

"William Lobb" produces a fantastic splash of purple-crimson on a vigorous plant which is sometime grown as a climber. The blooms, large for a Moss rose, are produced in small clusters in mid-summer. The plant has the typical attributes of a Moss, with heavily mossed stems and a rich scent. This is a good plant for the back of the border, to appear as a surprise when in full flower.

Type	Moss
Breeder	Laffay, France 1855
Parentage	Unknown
Synonyms	"Duchesse d'Istrie", "Old Velvet Moss"

WILLIAM'S DOUBLE YELLOW ▶

A rose with historical connections, "William's Double Yellow" is one of the best of the Scotch roses which enjoyed much popularity 200 years ago. The medium-sized, bright yellow double blooms, which have a pleasing fragrance, are produced early in the season. The shrub has typical fern-like foliage.

Type	Scotch
Origin	Introduced in 1824
Synonyms	"The Yellow Rose of Texas", "Harison's Yellow", "Prince Charlie's Rose"

MODERN SHRUB ROSES

Certain types of rose can be encouraged to develop into fairly
large, rounded shrubs, maturing at a height of about 6–8ft (1.8–
2.4m). They could be described as Floribundas which are not
pruned. All the plants in this group will produce plenty of flowers
throughout summer and autumn. To encourage this an extra feed
is recommended in late spring or early summer – they will respond
magnificently, particularly if you are meticulous about
dead-heading after the first flush of flowers to encourage
continuous growth.

◀ ALL THAT JAZZ

A beautiful coral-salmon blend, the large open flowers, produced in clusters, make a dazzling new contribution to the garden. The damask scent is a bonus. The dark green, glossy foliage is healthy. The plant has the appeal of an old-fashioned rose bush.

Breeder	Twomy, USA 1991
Parentage	Unknown
Awards	All-America Rose Selection 1992
Synonyms	"Twoadvance"

◀ BONICA

This very free-flowering pure pink rose has a unique place in the history of gardening as the first shrub rose to win an All-America Rose Selection Award. The beautiful clusters of medium-sized flowers have a moderate scent. The habit is slightly arching. When planted in groups it produces a bold splash of colour.

Breeder	Meilland, France 1981
Parentage	(*Rosa sempervirens* x "Mlle Marthe Carron") x "Picasso"
Awards	Certificate of Merit, Belfast 1985; All-America Rose Selection 1987
Synonyms	"Bonica Meidiland", "Meidomonac", "Bonica 82"

CAREFREE WONDER ▶

This beautiful shrub bears clusters of pretty pink, medium-sized flowers which are pale pink on the outside. The medium-sized plants have green glossy foliage. The flowers are lightly scented.

Breeder Meilland, France 1991
Parentage Unknown
Awards All-America Rose Selection 1991
Synonyms "Meipitac"

GOLDEN WINGS ▲

The large, single, light yellow blooms with their moderate scent produce a most delicate effect on a perfectly formed, round shrub about 5ft (1.5m) tall. When systematically dead-headed after the first flush of flowers it will produce a succession of colourful blooms.

Breeder Shepherd, USA 1956
Parentage "Soeur Thérèse" x (*Rosa pimpinellifolia altaica* x "Ormiston Roy")
Awards None
Synonyms None

GRAHAM THOMAS ▼

The finest yellow shrub from the breeding house of the new English Roses, many people would say "Graham Thomas" is the most popular rose of this type. The very rich yellow, medium-sized flowers have a wonderful tea rose fragrance and are produced on long stems which make it useful for flower arranging.

Breeder David Austin, UK 1983
Parentage "Charles Austin" x ("Iceberg" x seedling)
Awards None
Synonyms "Ausmas"

MARY ROSE

The very large double blooms of deep rose pink have an affinity with the source of so many of the new English Roses, the Damasks. The fragrance is pronounced. The plant grows into a medium-sized shrub.

Breeder	David Austin, UK 1983
Parentage	Seedling x "The Friar"
Awards	None
Synonyms	"Ausmary", "Country Marilou"

◀ STRECH JOHNSON

This rose produces an amazing display of colour. The large clusters of medium-sized flowers are orange-scarlet with a white rim and a yellow base, and light yellow on the reverse. It is sometimes classified as a Floribunda but if it is lightly pruned it will make an excellent shrub.

Breeder	McGredy, New Zealand 1988
Parentage	"Sexy Rexy" x "Maestro"
Awards	Gold Medal, Royal National Rose Society 1988; Golden Thorn, The Hague 1993
Synonyms	"Macfirwal", "Rock 'n Roll", "Tango"

$\mathscr{H}$YBRID $\mathscr{T}$EA $\mathscr{R}$OSES

Hybrid Teas and Floribundas are the familiar modern bush roses. The introduction of the large-flowered Hybrid Tea in 1867 with "La France" revolutionized rose growing and made the rose the astonishing success that it is today. Hybrid Teas have beautiful, elegantly pointed blooms on good long stems. The colour range is almost limitless and, contrary to some assumptions, there are more scented varieties now than ever before. The Hybrid Tea is generally planted in formal beds, where it has no peer in the garden. It can also provide colour when planted in groups in mixed herbaceous borders. The bushes need pruning in the early spring and benefit from an annual feed.

BARBARA BUSH ▶

Chosen by the former First Lady of the USA, the coral and ivory blooms have a high petal count which makes them equally beautiful in the garden or in a flower arrangement. They have a light fragrance. The handsome, dark green foliage provides a good foil to the flowers. The plant is vigorous.

Breeder Warriner, USA 1990
Parentage Unknown
Awards None
Synonyms "Jacbush"

   3·9

BRIDE'S DREAM ▼

The perfectly shaped, high pointed blooms make this a variety which is as popular on the show bench as in the garden. The pale pink fowers will often turn almost white in the hot sun. A vigorous bush with medium green foliage, it may need some protection from disease.

Breeder Kordes, Germany 1985
Parentage Unknown
Awards None
Synonyms "Koroyness", "Fairy Tale", "Märchenkonigen"

   3-10

COLOR MAGIC ▼

The long, pointed blooms of this rose are apricot to ivory pink with deep rose undertones. They have a slight fragrance. The foliage is a medium green and the plant is very tall.

Breeder Warriner, USA 1978
Parentage Unknown
Awards All-America Rose Selection 1978
Synonyms "Jacmag"

   3-10

DOUBLE DELIGHT ▶

Voted the world's favourite rose in 1985, "Double Delight" is generally accepted as the finest bicoloured rose in the garden today. The colour is a stunning creamy white with a crimson carmine flush. The perfectly formed, large flowers are renowned for their heady perfume and are produced on a plant with a branching habit. It may need protection from disease.

Breeder	Swim/Ellis 1977
Parentage	"Granada" x "Garden Party"
Awards	Many world-wide, including All-America Rose Selection 1977
Synonyms	"Andeli"

◀ ELINA

This rose was slow to gain public recognition but is now accepted as one of the finest Hybrid Teas introduced in recent years. The magnificent dark green foliage and vigorous stout plant habit contribute to a robust bush. The large, light yellow, perfectly shaped blooms have a moderate scent.

Breeder	Dickson, Northern Ireland 1985
Parentage	"Nana Mouskouri" x "Lolita"
Awards	Gold Medals, Germany 1987 and New Zealand 1989
Synonyms	"Dicjana", "Peaudouce"

FIRST PRIZE

For all its "middle age" this lovely pink rose with ivory tints still ranks as the classic show rose of the USA. The perfect high centre and large strong stems make it a great favourite. Its dislike of rain and disease susceptibility have discouraged its use in Europe.

Breeder Boerner, USA 1970
Parentage "Enchantment" seedling x "Golden Masterpiece" seedling
Awards All-America Rose Selection 1970
Synonyms None

   3-10

JUST JOEY

The dark green foliage, tinted with red when young, adds to the attractions of this lovely rose. The buff-orange, well-scented blooms can grow large if the plant is fed well. The slightly serrated petals are a novel feature.

Breeder Cants, UK 1972
Parentage "Fragrant Cloud" x "Dr A. J. Verhage"
Awards Many world-wide, including James Mason Medal, UK 1986
Synonyms None

   3-10

KEEPSAKE

An extremely disease-resistant, vigorous plant, "Keepsake" bears rich pink blooms which are large and well formed. With good feeding it will produce excellent exhibition-sized flowers which are very weather resistant.

Breeder Kordes, Germany 1981
Parentage Seedling x "Red Planet"
Awards Gold Medal, Portland 1987; Trial Ground Certificate, Royal National Rose Society 1980
Synonyms "Kormalda", "Esmeralda"

   3-10

MARIJKE KOOPMAN

A bright satiny prink turning to a rich pink, the blooms of this rose are large and it has gained many awards on the show bench. The fragrance and handsome foliage make it a popular variety.

Breeder Fryers, UK 1979
Parentage Unknown
Awards Gold Medal, The Hague 1978
Synonyms None

◀ MISTER LINCOLN

Huge, dark red roses have always been in demand and this variety has been a favourite for many years. The dark velvety blooms, paling slightly in the centre, have a wonderful fragrance. The strong upright growth is well clothed in dark green foliage.

Breeder Swim & Weeks, USA 1964
Parentage "Chrysler Imperial" x "Charles Mallerin"
Awards All-America Rose Selection 1965
Synonyms None

OLYMPIAD ▶

The bright red blooms of "Olympiad" are produced on long stems which make it good for cutting. Tremendously free flowering, this variety enjoys hot sunny weather, when it appears to gain in brilliance. It was the official rose of the Los Angeles Olympic games.

Breeder McGredy, New Zealand 1983
Parentage Unknown
Awards All-America Rose Selection 1984; Gold Medal, Portland 1985
Synonyms "Macauk", "Olympiade"

◀ PARADISE

Any rose with pretentions to being described as a blue rose will inevitably attract publicity. Its flowers are basically lavender, with heavy overtones of shocking pink magenta. The medium-sized blooms have a pleasing fragrance and are produced on a short, robust plant.

Breeder Weeks, USA 1978
Parentage Unknown
Awards All-America Rose Selection 1979; Gold Medal, Portland 1979
Synonyms "Wezeip", "Burning Sun"

PASCALI ▲

"Pascali" was voted the world's favourite rose in 1991, an unusual distinction for a white rose. White is a difficult colour to sell and it says much for this robust cultivar that it has maintained its popularity for so long. The dark green foliage is healthy and there is a modest scent.

Breeder	Lens, Belgium 1963
Parentage	"Queen Elizabeth" x "White Butterfly"
Awards	Many world-wide, including All-America Rose Selection 1969
Synonyms	"Lenip", "Blanche Pasca"

PEACE ▲

Described as the most famous rose in the world, "Peace" was voted the world's favourite rose 20 years ago. The large yellow blooms are tinged with pink as they age. The plant is robust and vigorous with luxuriant deep green foliage. It tolerates a wide variety of climates.

Breeder	Meilland, France 1942
Parentage	Seedling x "Margaret McGredy"
Awards	Many world-wide
Synonyms	"Gioia", "Gloria Dei", "Mme A. Meilland"

◀ PRISTINE

"Pristine" is an American rose which is universally recognized. The elegant, pinky white blooms have a pleasing fragrance. The strong, dark green leathery foliage is a perfect contrast.

Breeder	Warriner, USA 1978
Parentage	"White Masterpiece" x "First Prize"
Awards	Fragrance Medal, Royal National Rose Society 1979
Synonyms	"Jacpicol"

SHEER BLISS ▶

The beautiful, pastel, classically shaped blooms with creamy pink undertones have a strong sweet scent. This medium-sized plant is rapidly gaining a reputation as a tough rose which can withstand extremes of temperature.

Breeder Warriner, USA 1985
Parentage Unknown
Awards All-America Rose Selection 1987; Gold Medal, Japan 1984
Synonyms "Jactro"

◀ SHEER ELEGANCE

This produces large blooms in a blend of pinks with a classic form and light fragrance. The vigorous bush has long stems and dark green foliage. It is rapidly becoming a favourite on the show bench.

Breeder Twomy, USA 1989
Parentage Unknown
Awards All-America Rose Selection 1991
Synonyms "Twobe"

TOUCH OF CLASS

A coral pink blend with medium-sized blooms that have a slight fragrance, this is accepted as the top showing rose in the USA. The long pointed blooms are produced on good straight stems with healthy dark green foliage.

Breeder	Kriloff, France 1984
Parentage	Unknown
Awards	All-America Rose Selection 1986; Gold Medal, Portland 1988
Synonyms	"Kricaro", "Marechale Leclerc"

TOURNAMENT OF ROSES

This medium-height plant is very free flowering and is sometimes classed as a Floribunda. It produces coral buds that turn a soft pink as they age. The leaves are dark and glossy, and the stems are a good length.

Breeder	Warriner, USA 1988
Parentage	Unknown
Awards	All-America Rose Selection 1989
Synonyms	"Jacienta", "Berkley Poesie"

ℱLORIBUNDAS

The development of the modern rose was primarily concerned with production of large blooms with a classical form. Then in the early 1930s the Danish breeder Svend Poulsen conceived the idea of bush roses producing clusters of flowers. These first varieties, called Poulsen roses, were vigorous but lacked the range of colours in vogue in Hybrid Teas. Since the early 1940s, however, great strides have been made in plant style, colour and continuity of flowering. Today, cluster-flowered roses are very popular and because of their spray form can give a greater display of colour for much longer than Hybrid Teas. Their close affinity to Hybrid Tea bushes means that they are cultivated and pruned in exactly the same way. There is more variation in height, however, and care must be taken when choosing varieties.

AMBER QUEEN ▶

A very successful rose, this has gained many awards throughout the world. The relatively large blooms of pure amber have a good scent. The foliage is a very dark green. It is a good bedding rose.

Breeder Harkness, UK 1984
Parentage "Southampton" x "Typhoon"
Awards Many, including All-America Rose Selection 1988
Synonyms "Haroony", "Prinz Eugen von Savoyen"

    3-10

ANISLEY DICKSON ▼

A Floribunda with an outstanding output of flowers, the clusters of deep rosy salmon or warm coral generate a splash of colour. The medium-green foliage is disease resistant and contributes to a good garden variety which is also useful for cutting.

Breeder Dickson, Northern Ireland 1983
Parentage "Coventry Cathedral" x "Memento"
Awards President's International Trophy, Royal National Rose Society 1984
Synonyms "Dickimond", "Dicky", "Münchner Kindl"

    3-10

CLASS ACT ▼

The dark, glossy green foliage is a perfect foil for the creamy white buds which develop into snowy white blooms. The plant will sometimes grow into quite a large bush.

Breeder Warriner, USA 1988
Parentage Unknown
Awards All-America Rose Selection 1989
Synonyms "Jacare", "First Class", "White Magic"

    3-9

EUROPEANA

Very heavy clusters of rich, dark-red medium-sized blooms hang over in a form reminiscent of the old garden roses. The foliage is a deep purply green and an asset to any garden. It is prone to mildew.

Breeder	De Ruiter, Holland 1963
Parentage	"Ruth Leuwerik" x "Rosemary Rose"
Awards	All-America Rose Selection 1968; Gold Medals, The Hague 1962 and Portland 1970
Synonyms	None

◀ HANNAH GORDON

A marvellous blend of colours, the superb blooms of this rose are ivory edged with cherry pink. The abundant, dark green leaves complement the blooms perfectly. This is a vigorous plant with a good health record.

Breeder	Kordes, Germany 1983
Parentage	Seedling x "Bordure"
Awards	Trial Ground Certificate, Royal National Rose Society 1983
Synonyms	"Korweiso", "Raspberry Ice"

ICEBERG ▶

Probably the freest flowering rose that has ever been bred, "Iceberg" must be very close to continuous flowering. Pure white flowers are carried in large clusters on a vigorous bush with pale green foliage. The large trusses have a pleasing fragrance.

Breeder	Kordes, Germany 1958
Parentage	"Robin Hood" x "Virgo"
Awards	Gold Medal, Royal National Rose Society 1958; World's Favourite Rose 1985
Synonyms	"Fée de Neiges", "Schneeswittchen"

◀ MELODY MAKER

A bushy plant, "Melody Maker" produces high-quality blooms of light vermillion in clusters of medium size. The plant is average in height and makes an ideal subject for bedding.

Breeder	Dickson, Northern Ireland 1991
Parentage	Seedling of "Anisley Dickson"
Awards	Rose of the Year 1991
Synonyms	"Dicqueen"

NEW YEAR ▲

An apricot yellow rose with such high-quality blooms that it is sometimes rated as a Hybrid Tea. The dark leathery foliage is a perfect foil to a beautiful rose with a sweet fragrance.

Breeder McGredy, New Zealand 1983
Parentage Unknown
Awards All-America Rose Selection 1987
Synonyms "Macneweya", "Arcadian"

PURPLE TIGER ▲

The most astonishing colour combination of recent years, this rose is quite theatrical in appearance. The large purple blooms have pale pink stripes. It needs some protection from black spot.

Breeder Christensen, USA 1991
Parentage Unknown
Awards None
Synonyms "Jacpur", "Impressionist"

ORANGES AND LEMONS ▶

This startling variety has unique colouring and presages a completely new dimension in rose breeding. The large double blooms which occur in clusters are orange, striped with scarlet. The coppery-coloured foliage is an excellent complement to this new variety.

Breeder McGredy, New Zealand 1993
Parentage "New Year" x Seedling
Awards Trial Ground Certificate, Royal National Rose Society 1991
Synonyms None

SEXY REXY

The very large trusses of camellia-shaped blooms are pure pink. "Sexy Rexy" is a bedding variety with exceptional bloom production and a very tough constitution. It is popular world-wide.

Breeder McGredy, New Zealand 1984
Parentage "Seaspray" x "Dreaming"
Awards Certificate of Merit, Royal National Rose Society 1985
Synonyms "Macrexy", "Heckenzauber"

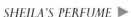

SHEILA'S PERFUME

A robust plant with a strong constitution, "Sheila's Perfume" has handsome foliage and stout stems. The splendidly scented, big blooms are bright red and yellow, and of Hybrid Tea quality.

Breeder Sheridan, UK 1982
Parentage "Peer Gynt" x ["Daily Sketch" x ("Paddy McGredy" x "Prima Ballerina")]
Awards Many world-wide for fragrance
Synonyms "Harsherry"

SIMPLICITY ▶

A free-flowering variety, "Simplicity" has been described as a pink "Iceberg" because of the abundance of flowers, but this is slightly flattering for a rose which is a hedging plant in many gardens. Its lush foliage and purity of colour make it outstanding and it has been planted in large numbers.

Breeder Warriner, USA 1978
Parentage Unknown
Awards Gold Medal, New Zealand 1976
Synonyms "Jacink"

◀ *SPANISH SHAWL*

This is one of Sam McGredy's more flamboyant Floribundas from the breeding line of the "hand-painted" roses. The very showy blooms have a white eye blending into scarlet and the tips of the petals are cream. A startling mixture that produces clusters of large flowers on a medium-sized bush.

Breeder McGredy, New Zealand 1980
Parentage Seedling x ["Evelyn Fison" x ("Orange Sweetheart" x Fruhlingsmorgen)]
Awards Certificate of Merit, Royal National Rose Society, 1977; Gold Medal, New Zealand 1981
Synonyms "Macspash", "Kobold", "Sue Lawley"

SUN FLARE ▶

The flowers, with their spicy perfume, are variously described as bright yellow or lemon yellow, and are set off by glossy foliage. The plant is low growing, with a slightly spreading habit.

Breeder	Warriner, USA 1981
Parentage	Unknown
Awards	All-America Rose Selection 1983
Synonyms	"Jacjem", "Sunflare"

SUNSPRITE ▼

The deep, unfading clear yellow clusters are produced on a free-flowering bush of medium height. The strong fragrance is a bonus for a yellow Floribunda. "Sunsprite" is very popular and grown in vast numbers.

Breeder	Kordes, Germany 1974
Parentage	"Friedrich Worlein" x "Spanish Sun"
Awards	Gold Medal, Baden Baden 1972
Synonyms	"Korresia", "Fresia"

THE TIMES ROSE ▼

The very dark crimson flowers are produced in big clusters. The plant is upright in habit, flower production is tremendous and the resistance to disease is phenomenal. The very dark, glossy foliage is an extra asset.

Breeder	Kordes, Germany 1984
Parentage	"Tornado" x "Redgold"
Awards	President's International Trophy, Royal National Rose Society 1982
Synonyms	"Korpeahn", "Carl Philip", "Christian IV", "Mariandel"

TRUMPETER

Medium-sized, vivid scarlet-orange trusses are produced in abundance on a short plant. Glossy foliage which is disease free makes for a high-quality bedding rose.

Breeder McGredy, New Zealand 1977
Parentage "Satchmo" x seedling
Awards Many world-wide
Synonyms "Mactrum"

WISHING

The deep salmon-pink flowers are produced in neatly spaced clusters. The medium-sized blooms have a shining radiance. The medium green bushy growth contributes to a robust plant.

Breeder Dickson, Northern Ireland 1985
Parentage "Silver Jubilee" x "Bright Smile"
Awards Certificate of Merit, Royal National Rose Society 1984; Certificate of Merit, Belfast and Glasgow 1987
Synonyms "Dickerfuffle", "Georgie Girl"

$\mathscr{P}$ATIO AND $\mathscr{M}$INIATURE $\mathscr{R}$OSES

The miniaturized rose evolved at the beginning of this century
when a small plant (*Rosa roulettii*) was discovered in Europe.
The blood lines of this valuable plant were subsequently used in
breeding a whole host of new varieties. Varying in height from 6in
(15cm) to 12in (30cm) they quickly became popular, particularly
on the Continent and in the USA. They are very useful for planting
up garden pots and in small miniaturized garden schemes. Starting
from a very ordinary pink their colour range now equals that of
any other type.

Recently, breeders have made a concerted effort to produce the
small leaves and flowers on a slightly bigger plant and thus the
patio rose has evolved – a very free-flowering plant about 18in
(45cm) to 24in (60cm) high but with the delightful characteristics
of the miniature rose. There is now the possibility that
miniaturized flowers and leaves will be extended to shrubs.
Both types have the same wide spectrum of colour as in other
types of rose. Their demands as a garden plant are also identical:
plenty of light, annual pruning and regular feeding.

ANNA FORD

This was one of the first patio roses. The small, semi-double blooms grow in very neat clusters, on a bushy plant. The flowers are orange-red with a yellow base.

Breeder Harkness, UK 1980
Parentage "Southampton" x "Darling Flame"
Awards Many, including President's International Trophy, Royal National Rose Society 1981
Synonyms "Harpiccolo"

DRUMMER BOY

A round bush with deep, bright crimson flowers, "Drummer Boy" is highly productive in a long flowering season. The plant is effective both as a bedding rose or as a small hedge, producing a bright splash of colour.

Breeder Harkness, UK 1987
Parentage Seedling x "Red Sprite"
Awards None
Synonyms "Harvacity"

GENTLE TOUCH ►

This was the first patio rose to gain popular recognition, when it was voted rose of the year in 1986. The pale pink flowers are perfectly formed and the bush is highly productive.

Breeder Dickson, Northern Ireland 1986
Parentage "Liverpool Echo" x ("Woman's Own" x "Memento")
Awards Rose of the Year 1986
Synonyms "Diclulu"

GINGERNUT ►

Pretty orange flowers with a red reverse which are pleasantly fragrant are produced on a compact bush. The small semi-glossy leaves are highly resistant to disease.

Breeder Cocker, UK 1989
Parentage ("Sabina" x "Circus") x "Darling Flame"
Awards None
Synonyms "Coccrazy"

GREEN DIAMOND

This miniature can justifiably claim to have a unique colour for a rose. The very compact plant seldom grows more than 9in (23cm) high and is constantly smothered in exquisite, very pale green blooms. A very useful novelty rose that contributes well to small flower arrangements.

Breeder	Moore, USA 1975
Parentage	Seedling x "Sheri Anne"
Awards	None
Synonyms	None

    3-10

HOLY TOLEDO

A pretty, vigorous, patio rose which is widely grown around the world. The cupped blooms have a perfect form, coming in small clusters on a plant about 18in (46cm) high. The glowing apricot flower colour is complemented by dark green glossy foliage.

Breeder	Christensen, USA 1978
Parentage	Unknown
Awards	None
Synonyms	"Arobril"

   3-10

LITTLE BO-PEEP ▼

"Little Bo-Peep" can well be described as a truly miniature shrub rose. The round plants are about 10in (25cm) high and a bush with a similar radius will produce beautiful cushions of tiny, pale pink flowers. The foliage is equally small but the plant is very free.

Breeder	Poulsen, Denmark 1992
Parentage	"Caterpillar" x Seedling
Awards	Presidents International Trophy, Royal National Rose Society 1991
Synonyms	"Poullen"

MINILIGHTS ▲

This is a cheerful little plant covered in single yellow flowers, with attractive shiny green foliage. The plant is about 12in (30cm) high and spreads to 20in (50cm) across.

Breeder	Dickson, Northern Ireland 1988
Parentage	"White Spray" x "Bright Smile"
Awards	Trial Ground Certificate, Royal National Rose Society 1985
Synonyms	"Dicmoppet", "Goldfacher", "Mini Lights"

MAGIC CAROUSEL ▶

An extremely free-flowering miniature with an abundance of moderately violet-scented blooms. The small high-centred flowers are white-edged with carmine crimson and the plant grows to about 12in (30cm) high.

Breeder	Moore, USA 1972
Parentage	"Little Darling" x "Westmount"
Awards	None
Synonyms	"Moorcar", "Morrousel"

◀ NEW BEGINNING

Orange-red blooms are borne continuously, on a reliable plant which becomes an excellent low-growing hedge of about 12–15in (30–38cm). It makes a beautiful contribution to the garden.

Breeder Saville, USA 1988
Parentage Unknown
Awards All-America Rose Selection 1989
Synonyms "Savabeg"

    4-9

◀ PEEK-A-BOO

Apricot or coppery orange blooms turn to a pretty pink as they age. The flowers are produced with great continuity. The plant is very vigorous, growing to about 24in (60cm). This is a patio rose of the highest calibre.

Breeder Dickson, Northern Ireland 1981
Parentage "Memento" x "Nozomi"
Awards Certificate of Merit, Royal National Rose Society 1981
Synonyms "Dicgrow", "Brass Ring"

   4-9

PRIDE 'N JOY

A very vigorous patio rose, this can occasionally grow to 3ft (90cm). The bright orange blooms have a yellow reverse. The rounded bush has matt green foliage and is a marvellous addition to the type.

Breeder	Warriner, USA 1991
Parentage	Unknown
Awards	All-American Rose Selection 1992
Synonyms	"Jacmo"

    4-9

RAINBOW'S END

A pretty miniature, this reliable variety has proved very successful and popular both on the show bench and in the garden. The deep yellow blooms turn red at the tips in full sunlight as they age. The leaves are small, dark green and glossy.

Breeder	Saville, USA 1984
Parentage	"Rise 'N Shine" x "Water Color"
Awards	None
Synonyms	"Savalife"

    4-9

SWEET DREAM ▶

This popular cultivar gained instant recognition as a very reliable patio rose. Voted rose of the year in 1988, it is now the most widely grown of this type. A vigorous, free-flowering plant produces lovely, frilly peachy-apricot flowers with a light scent.

Breeder	Fryers, UK 1988
Parentage	Unknown
Awards	Rose of the Year 1988
Synonyms	"Fryminicot", "Sweet Dreams"

    3-9

◀ TOP MARKS

When this variety was judged at the Royal National Rose Society trials two years ago it is reputed to have gained the highest points ever for a patio rose. The vivid, orange-vermilion, double blooms are borne in clusters on a compact bush.

Breeder	Fryer, UK 1992
Parentage	Unknown
Awards	Gold Medal, Royal National Rose Society, 1990; Gold Medal, Dublin 1991
Synonyms	"Fryministar"

    3-10

$\mathcal{G}$ROUND-COVER AND $\mathcal{L}$ANDSCAPE $\mathcal{R}$OSES

The idea that the rose can contribute to the environment when
planted along highways, in new towns and in difficult parts of the
garden is relatively new, although the plant form has been known
for some time. Ground-cover roses have been introduced during
the last 20 years and are enabling the genus to be grown in the
most unlikely situations. Basically, the criteria are the ability to
produce a flush or flushes of flowers on plants which do not need
pruning, are disease free and have very tough constitutions.
The first of the modern ground-cover roses were rather large for
small gardens and only produced one crop of flowers a year.
The recent introductions are much smaller, ranging from 24in
(60cm) to 48in (1.2m) across, and have the ability to flower
recurrently. In common with all other roses they need feeding but
are tolerant of semi-shade.

FLOWER CARPET

An extremely prolific rose, "Flower Carpet" has received tremendous publicity because of its impact in gardens. The large trusses of double pink flowers are very attractive and provide colour over a long period. The plentiful bright glossy foliage is an added bonus. The plant will spread to 4ft (1.2m)

Breeder	Noack, Germany 1989
Parentage	"Immensee" x "Amanda"
Awards	Gold Medal, The Hague 1990
Synonyms	"Noatrum", "Blooming Carpet", "Heidetraum"

◀ MAGIC CARPET

Described as a beautiful cover for difficult areas, the 2in (5cm) lavender blooms with their spicy fragrance are produced profusely in clusters on a vigorous and splendid plant.

Breeder	Zary/Warriner, USA 1992
Parentage	Unknown
Awards	None
Synonyms	"Jaclover"

MAINAUFEUER

Deep red flowers are produced on a new type of ground-cover rose. The plant will spread to about 6ft (1.8m) and cover big areas with a mass of colour. A healthy plant, it needs little maintenance.

Breeder Kordes, Germany 1991
Parentage Unknown
Awards Gold Medal, Baden Baden 1991
Synonyms "Kortemma", "Chilterns", "Fiery Sunsation"

     3-10

◀ NOZOMI

One of the earliest of the "miniature" ground covers, "Nozomi" is equally good as a small climber or weeping tree rose. The very small, pinky white flowers are produced in profusion in the summer. The foliage is composed of very small shiny leaflets. A mature plant is a memorable sight.

Breeder Onodera, Japan 1968
Parentage "Fairy Princess" x "Sweet Fairy"
Awards None
Synonyms "Heideröslein"

    4-9

PEARL MEDILAND

The Mediland family of ground-cover roses, originating in France, has become very popular in the USA. Noted for their long season of blooming and disease-resistant foliage, these roses make splendid plants about 24in (60cm) high and 5ft (1.5m) across. This particular variety has dainty pastel blooms of pink and pearl.

Breeder   Meilland, France 1979
Parentage   Unknown
Awards   None
Synonyms   "Meiplaten", "Perle Meillandécor"

   4-9

RAUBRITTER

This variety of rose was born before its time. A mature plant is a mound of flower about 3ft (90cm) high and 6ft (1.8m) across. The small, globular flowers are produced in masses in mid-summer and are set off by dark greyish-green foliage.

Breeder   Kordes, Germany 1936
Parentage   "Daisy Hill" x "Solarium"
Awards   None
Synonyms   None

   3-10

RALPH'S CREEPER

A red and yellow bicolour which will spread to about 6ft (1.8m) but only grows 18in (45cm) high, "Ralph's Creeper" will cover big areas with mass planting and needs very little maintenance. It has small, glossy leaves and an apple blossom scent.

Breeder   Moore, USA 1987
Parentage   Unknown
Awards   None
Synonyms   "Morpapplay", "Creepy", "Highveld Sun"

   4-10

RED BLANKET

An extremely prolific variety, "Red Blanket" has become very well established. The semi-double, small red flowers are produced on a plant about 3ft (90cm) tall and 5ft (1.5m) across and create an amazing carpet of colour. The foliage is disease free and lasts well into the winter.

Breeder Ilsink, Holland 1979
Parentage "Yesterday" x seedling
Awards None
Synonyms "Intercell"

SCARLET MEDILAND

This variety is distinct from the other Mediland types. The large clusters are comprised of small, double scarlet blooms. There is a large flush in early summer, followed by intermittent flowers. The plant is very hardy and disease resistant.

Breeder Meilland, France 1987
Parentage Unknown
Awards Certificate of Merit, Glasgow 1989
Synonyms "Meikrotal", "Scarlet Meillandécor"

SNOW CARPET ▶

A miniature ground cover, "Snow Carpet" will also make a good tree rose. It is the very first of this type, with myriads of very small double white flowers. The plant will mature at about 2ft (60cm) wide but only 6in (15cm) high.

Breeder McGredy, New Zealand 1980
Parentage "New Penny" x "Temple Bells"
Awards Gold Medal, Baden Baden 1982
Synonyms "Maccarpe", "Blanche Neige"

◀ THE FAIRY

An old favourite, this has now found its niche. Flowering from mid-summer to autumn, the very double, small pink flowers make clusters which droop languidly. The plant produces a mound of flowers 3ft (90cm) high and 4ft (1.2m) across.

Breeder Bentall, UK 1932
Parentage "Paul Crampel" x "Lady Gay"
Awards None
Synonyms "Feerie"

CLIMBERS AND RAMBLERS

Historically, these forms of rose are of recent introduction, not appearing in gardens until the late eighteenth century, after the discovery of *Rosa wichuraiana* in the Far East and its appearance in Europe in 1790. By 1900 there was a plethora of rampant ramblers, many of which are still popular.

Until the early 1950s the climbing roses were mostly mutations of bush varieties and were all summer flowering. Since then, hybridists have bred recurrent flowering forms with the bonus of a greater colour range.

It is convenient to categorize all roses which climb or ramble as four distinct types. Climbers, recurrent flowering are generally modern varieties while climbers, summer flowering are usually mutations of bush roses. Ramblers, recurrent flowering are the modern varieties and ramblers, summer flowering are the old favourites.

ALOHA

A shrubby climber, "Aloha" has gained world-wide recognition with its wonderful fragrance and ability to grow in sunless situations. The double blooms of rose and salmon pink are produced throughout summer and autumn.

Breeder Boerner, USA 1949
Parentage "Mercedes Gallart" x "New Dawn"
Awards None
Synonyms None

    3-9

AMERICA

An abundance of salmon-pink, medium-sized flowers are produced on a vigorous plant of medium height. The heavy clove fragrance of the blooms is an added attraction. The foliage is a clear dark green and disease resistant.

Breeder Warriner, USA 1976
Parentage "Fragrant Cloud" x "Tradition"
Awards All-America Rose Selection 1976
Synonyms "Jacclam"

   4-9

ALTISSIMO

This is probably the largest single rose (five petals) growing in gardens around the world today. The brilliant scarlet petals with their prominent yellow stamens are produced on a vigorous plant which can reach 40ft (12m) and will flower throughout summer and autumn.

Breeder Delbard-Chabert, France 1966
Parentage "Ténor" x seedling
Awards None
Synonyms None

   4-9

AMERICAN PILLAR

This is an old favourite. Large clusters of carmine single flowers with white eyes are produced in great profusion in mid-summer. A rampant variety, it has tough glossy foliage which nevertheless may fall prey to mildew in the autumn. It needs dead-heading to encourage new growth.

Breeder Van Fleet, USA 1902
Parentage (*Rosa wichuraiana* x *Rosa setigera*) x a red Hybrid Perpetual
Awards None
Synonyms None

    3·9

◀ BANKSIAN YELLOW

A climber for the warmer parts of the garden, "Banksian Yellow" is tremendously vigorous and some plants have grown to over 50ft (15m). It will produce an amazing display of colour in late spring. The very small, buttercup-yellow flowers are usually produced on old wood. There is a double white form, *Rosa banksiae alba-plena*.

Origin Discovered in China and introduced into Europe in about 1824
Synonyms *Rosa banksiae lutea*

    6-10

◀ BLAZE

An extremely free-flowering bright red climber, "Blaze" has a great following in the USA although it has never been popular in Europe. In many areas it will flower throughout summer and autumn. It is frequently used on fences, screens and pillars, to which it is ideally suited. There are reputedly several improvements, with the adjunct Superior or Improved.

Breeder	Kallay, USA 1932
Parentage	"Paul's Scarlet Climber" x "Gruss an Toplitz"
Awards	None
Synonyms	None

   3-9

◀ CLIMBING CECILE BRUNNER

A tremendous climber, this is a mutation of an early China rose. The exquisite miniature pink blooms are produced in great profusion. A mature plant will grow to 40ft (12m) and although classified as a summer flowerer it is highly productive in warm situations throughout the autumn.

Origin	Discovered by Hosp in 1894
Synonyms	Climbing Mlle Cecile Brunner

   4-9

CLIMBING PEACE ▲

This is the climbing form of the most famous rose ever introduced. The growth is both big and luxuriant and the blooms appear larger than the type. In some areas, particularly in gardens with a lot of shade, the plant is reluctant to produce flowers in abundance. This can be remedied by allowing old wood to accumulate and by "starving" the plant at the same time.

Origin Discovered by Brandy in 1980
Synonyms None

   3-9

DORTMUND ▲

A pretty crimson with a pronounced white eye, the single blooms are borne in clusters on a lax growth which must make it one of the few recurrent flowering ramblers. The dark green healthy foliage is very resistant to disease.

Breeder Kordes, Germany 1955
Parentage Seedling x *Rosa kordesii*
Awards None
Synonyms None

    3-9

CLIMBING QUEEN ELIZABETH ▶

A mutation from the type, this rose must be allowed to accumulate old wood which will produce intermittent blooms. The flowers are well shaped and have the characteristic large pink blooms with a slight scent. They are very useful as cut flowers.

Origin Discovered by Whisler in 1957
Synonyms "Climbing The Queen Elizabeth Rose"

    3-10

DUBLIN BAY ▶

A blood-red climber of moderate height, this rose is equally at home as a shrub. The large, bright crimson blooms are well shaped and produced in small clusters. It is very good on walls and low fences. The glossy foliage is an added attraction.

Breeder McGredy, New Zealand 1976
Parentage "Bantry Bay" x "Altissimo"
Awards Many world-wide
Synonyms "Macdub"

◀ FOUNTAIN

A brilliant scarlet vigorous shrub in Europe, this doubles as a climber in the USA. It produces tremendously free-flowering, large semi-double blooms with an abundance of healthy, deep green foliage. It is probably the finest variety in this colour range.

Breeder Tantau, Germany 1970
Parentage Unknown
Awards President's International Trophy, Royal National Rose Society 1971
Synonyms "Fountaine", "Red Prince"

GOLDEN SHOWERS

Probably the most widely grown climber world-wide, "Golden Showers" produces large, semi-double golden-yellow blooms on long stems which are good for cutting. Because of its high flower production, time must be given to allow a good fabric to build up. Nevertheless, plants 15–20ft (4.5–6m) high and as wide are very common.

Breeder	Lammerts, USA 1957
Parentage	"Charlotte Armstrong" x "Capt. Thomas"
Awards	All-America Rose Selection 1957; Gold Medal, Portland 1957
Synonyms	None

HANDEL

A very beautiful climber, "Handel" produces ivory blooms with a fascinating rose pink flush towards the ends of the petals. It is highly productive and capable of covering a wall or a pillar to about 15ft (4.5m). The stems are strong and straight which makes it a good subject for cut flowers.

Breeder	McGredy, New Zealand 1965
Parentage	"Columbine" x "Heidelberg"
Awards	Many world-wide
Synonyms	"Macha", "Haendel"

JOSEPH'S COAT ▶

As the name implies, this rose is a gorgeous mixture of yellow, orange and cherry red. The clusters of medium to small semi-double flowers provide a feast of colour for a very long time. It needs dead-heading to encourage continuity of bloom.

Breeder Armstrong/Swim, USA 1969
Parentage "Buccaneer" x "Circus"
Awards Certificate of Merit, Royal National Rose Society 1964

Synonyms None

◀ *NEW DAWN*

An extremely free-flowering, very pale pink climber, "New Dawn" is widely grown world-wide. An historic rose, the parent of many modern climbers, it will grow in the most difficult situations. Although a mature plant will grow to 20ft (6m) it is probably more spectacular on fences and low-growing pergolas. The scent is just one of its many appealing properties.

Origin Discovered as a sport of Dr Van Fleet, Somerset Rose Nurseries in 1930
Synonyms "The New Dawn"

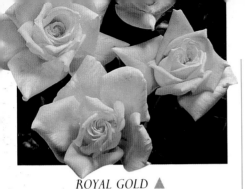

ROYAL GOLD

A moderate climber, "Royal Gold" has golden-yellow double blooms of Hybrid Tea quality. The scent is pleasant and the foliage a glossy deep green. It does best in a sheltered garden in full sun, where it consistently produces beautiful blooms.

Breeder	Morey, USA 1957
Parentage	"Climbing Goldilocks" x "Lydia"
Awards	None
Synonyms	None

    5-10

ZEPHIRINE DROUHIN

This has a unique niche in the world of roses as the thornless climber. The flowers are deep pink, and semi-double with an astonishing scent. The plant will grow to about 10ft (3m) and is equally happy in sun or shade. It sometimes needs protection from disease.

Breeder	Bizot, France 1868
Parentage	A Bourbon seedling
Awards	None
Synonyms	"Charles Bonnet"

   4-9

WEDDING DAY

A prodigious rambler, "Wedding Day" will grow to 50ft (15m) and is an ideal plant to grow through trees and cascade in a spectacular display in mid-summer. The large clusters of single white blooms with their prominent yellow stamens have a moderate scent. The shiny leaves and small yellow hips make for a superb plant.

Breeder	Stern, UK 1950
Parentage	*Rosa sinowilsonii* seedling
Awards	None
Synonyms	None

    3-10

TREE ROSES

Most roses are propagated on rootstock. This is because most modern cultivars do not grow particularly well if grown on their own roots and need the boost that a more vigorous rootstock can give. A tree rose is propagated on much the same principle but the stock itself is a long stem. The height from ground level to the point of union at the trunk varies. Thus a half standard measures 2ft (60cm) from the ground to the point of union, a full standard measures 3ft (90cm) and a shrub or weeping standard measures 4–5ft (1.2–1.5m).

Although most cultivars can be grown as tree roses, some do not appear to thrive. The most important factor is to recognize that tree roses must be well staked. They are not very winter hardy and so persistent cold temperatures will not suit them. Their great asset in the garden is that they give height to an otherwise flat bed or border. Pruning standards is done in much the same way as for their bush counterparts.

DOROTHY PERKINS

The naturally lax habit of many of the older ramblers has been used to great effect when propagated as "umbrella roses" or weeping standards. There are many of these types but few can equal the floriferousness of this variety. The long arms, fully clothed in masses of pink bloom, make a tremendous impact. Grown in sheltered areas, out of the wind, and well staked it will repay extra feeding with very little maintenance. It is customarily grown on a 5ft (1.5m) trunk.

Breeder Jackson & Perfins, USA 1901
Parentage *Rose wichuraiana* x "Mme Gabriel Luizet"
Awards None
Synonyms None

     4-9

FRAGRANT CLOUD

One of the advantages of growing a tree rose is that the gardener does not have to bend down to enjoy the fragrance. The scent from the large, dusky scarlet blooms of "Fragrant Cloud" is legendary and is there to be enjoyed throughout the summer.

Breeder Tautau, Germany 1963
Parentage Seedling x "Prima Ballerina"
Awards President's International Trophy, Royal National Rose Society 1964
Synonyms "Nuage Parfumé", "Duftwolke"

     4-9

ICEBERG

Floribundas can vary tremendously in height but the most successful make good rounded bushes. "Iceberg" is a natural and can give a new dimension to a rose bed or border with its visual impact.

Breeder Kordes, Germany 1958
Parentage "Robin Hood" x "Virgo"
Awards Gold Medal, Royal National Rose Society 1958; World's Favourite Rose 1985
Synonyms "Fée de Neiges", "Schneeswittchen"

    4-9

◀ NOZOMI

The introduction of the newer ground-cover roses has opened up a completely new concept of tree roses in the garden. Their naturally pendulous plant form means they are tailor made for many situations. "Nozomi" must be one of the most successful. With a trunk of about 4ft (1.2m), a mature plant will create an excellent display, with the fully clothed branches reaching almost to the ground. Apart from ample staking this variety needs virtually no maintenance and certainly no pruning.

Breeder Onodera, Japan 1968
Parentage "Fairy Princess" x "Sweet Fairy"
Awards None
Synonyms "Heideröslein"

   4-9

PEACE

Any rose variety which is grown as a tree rose must make a good head and have a rounded growth habit. Any rose that is tall and thin when grown as a bush will not be very satisfactory. Peace, with its robust growth, is an ideal subject and its luxuriant foliage is a bonus.

Breeder Meilland, France 1942
Parentage Seedling x "Margaret McGredy"
Awards Many world-wide
Synonyms "Gioia", "Gloria Dei", "Mme A. Meilland"

   4-9

THE FAIRY

The concept that shrub roses will make good tree roses is a relatively recent development. Shrub roses have been used before but with little success because of the limited range of available material. A tree rose of "The Fairy" is a memorable sight as its naturally lax habit makes for a well-shaped head which flowers throughout summer and autumn.

Breeder Bentall, UK 1932
Parentage "Paul Crampel" x "Lady Gay"
Awards None
Synonyms "Feerie"

    4-9

SWEET MAGIC

Most patio roses and the more vigorous miniatures make fascinating garden plants. Usually propagated on a 2ft (60cm) trunk, they are propagated for planting in pots and in small planting schemes. "Sweet Magic" has golden-orange flowers flushed with pink. They are double and slightly fragrant.

Breeder Dixon, UK 1987
Parentage "Peek-a-Boo" x "Bright Smile"
Awards Trial Ground Certificate, Royal National Rose Society 1986; Rose of the Year 1987
Synonyms "Dicmagic"

    5-9

INDEX

A

"All That Jazz" 32
"Aloha" 68
"Altissimo" 68
"Amber Queen" 45
"America" 68
"American Pillar" 69
"Andeli" 37
"Anisley Dickson" 45
"Anna Ford" 54
"Arcadian" 48
"Arobril" 56
"Ausmary" 34
"Ausmas" 33

B

"Banksian Yellow" 69
"Barbara Bush" 36
"Berkley Poesie" 43
"Blanc Double de
    Coubert" 23
"Blanche Neige" 66
"Blanche Pasca" 41
"Blaze" 70
"Blooming Carpet" 62
"Bonica" 32
"Brass Ring" 58
"Bride's Dream" 36
"Burning Sun" 40

C

"Cardinal de Richelieu"
    23
"Carefree Wonder" 33
"Carl Philip" 51
"Charles Bonnet" 75
"Charles de Mills" 23
"Chilterns" 63
"Christian IV" 51
"Class Act" 45
"Climbing Cecile Brunner"
    70
"Climbing Peace" 71
"Climbing Queen
    Elizabeth" 71
"Coccrazy" 55
"Color Magic" 36
"Common Moss" 24
"Communis" 24
"Country Marilou" 34
"Cuisse de Nymphe
    Emue" 25

D

"Dicgrow" 58
"Dicjana" 37
"Dickeruffle" 52
"Dickimond" 45
"Dicky" 45
"Diclulu" 55
"Dicmagic" 79
"Dicmoppet" 57
"Dicqueen" 47
"Dorothy Perkins" 77
"Dortmund" 71
"Double Delight" 37
"Drummer Boy" 54
"Dublin Bay" 72
"Duchesse d'Istrie" 30
"Duftwolke" 77

E

"Elina" 37
"Esmeralda" 38
"Europeana" 46

F

"The Fairy" 66; tree 79
"Fairy Tale" 36
"Fée de Neiges" 47, 78
"Ferdinand Pichard" 24
"Fiery Sunsation" 63
"First Class" 45
"First Prize" 38
"Flower Carpet" 62
"Fountain" 72
"Fragrant Cloud" 77
"Fresia" 51
"Fru Dagmar Hastrup" 24
"Fryminicot" 60
"Fryministar" 60

G

"Gentle Touch" 55
"Georgie Girl" 52
"Gingernut" 55
"Gioia" 41; tree 79
"Gloria Dei" 41, 79
Golden Rose of China 19
"Golden Showers" 73
"Golden Wings" 33
"Goldfacher" 57
"Graham Thomas" 33
"Great Maiden's Blush" 25
"Green Diamond" 56

H

"Handel" 73
"Hannah Gordon" 46
"Harison's Yellow" 30
"Haroony" 45
"Harpiccolo" 54
"Harsherry" 49
"Harvacity" 54
"Heckenzauber" 49
"Heideröslein" 63, 78
"Heidetraum" 62
"Highveld Sun" 64
"Holy Toledo" 56

I

"Iceberg" 47; tree 78
"Impressionist" 48
"Incarnata" 25

J

"Jacare" 45
"Jacbush" 36
"Jacclam" 68
"Jacienta" 43
"Jacink" 50
"Jacjem" 51
"Jaclover" 62
"Jacmag" 36
"Jacmo" 59
"Jacpicol"41
"Jacpur" 48
"Jactro" 42
"Joseph's Coat" 74
"Just Joey" 38

K

"Keepsake" 38
"Kormalda" 38
"Koroyness" 36

"Korpeahn" 51
"Korresia" 51
"Kortemma" 63
"Korweiso" 46
"Kricaro" 43

L

"La Reine Victoria" 25
"Lenip" 41
"Little Bo-Peep" 57

M

"Macauk" 40
"Macdub" 72
"Macfirwal" 34
"Macha" 73
"Macneweya" 48
"Macspash" 50
"Mactrum" 63
"Magic Carousel" 57
"Magic Carpet" 62
"Mainaufeuer" 63
"Märchenkonigen" 36
"Marechale Leclerc" 43
"Mariandel" 51
"Marijke Koopman" 39
"Mary Rose" 34
"Meidomonac" 32
"Meikrotal" 65
"Meipitac" 33
"Meiplaten" 64
"Melody Maker" 47
"Miller's Moss" 24
"Minilights" 57
"Mister Lincoln" 39
"Mme A. Meilland" 41, 79
"Mme Isaac Pereire" 26
"Mme Plantier" 26
"Moorcar" 57
"Morpapplay" 64
"Morrousel" 57
"Müncher Kindl" 45

N

"New Beginning" 58
"New Dawn" 74
"New Year" 48
"Noatrum" 62
"Nozomi" 63, 78
"Nuage Parfumé" 77

O

"Old Pink Moss" 24
"Old Velvet Moss" 30
"Olympiad" 40
"Oranges and Lemons" 48

P

"Paradise" 40
"Pascali" 41
"Paul Neyron" 27
"Peace" 41, 79
"Pearl Mediland" 64
"Peaudouce" 37
"Peek-a-Boo" 58
"Penelope" 27
"Pink Grootendorst" 28
"Poullen" 57
"Pride 'n Joy" 59
"Prince Charlie's Rose" 30
"Prinz Eugen von
    Savoyen" 45
"Pristine" 41
"Purple Tiger" 48

Q

"Queen of Violets" 28

R

"Rainbow's End" 59
"Ralph's Creeper" 64
"Raspberry Ice" 46
"Raubritter" 64
"Red Blanket" 65
"Red Prince" 72
"Reine des Violettes" 28
"Rock 'n Roll" 34
Rosa farreri persetosa 19
Rosa gallica versicolor 28
Rosa glauca 19
Rosa hugonis 19
Rosa longicuspis 20
Rosa moyesii geranium 20
Rosa mundi 28
Rosa omiensis
    pteracantha 21
Rosa rubrifolia 19
Rosa rugosa alba 29
Rosa sericea pteracantha 21
Rosa xanthia var.
    spontanea "Canary
    Bird" 21
Rosa x centifolia
    "Muscosa" 7, 24
"Roseraie de l'Hay 29
"Royal Gold" 75

S

"Savabeg" 58
"Savalife" 59
"Scarlet Mediland" 65
"Schneeswittchen" 78
"Sexy Rexy" 49
"Sheer Bliss" 42
"Sheer Elegance" 42
"Sheila's Perfume" 49
"Simplicity" 50
"Snow Carpet" 66
"Spanish Shawl" 50
"Strech Johnson" 34
"Sue Lawley" 50
"Sun Flare" 51
"Sunsprite" 51
"Sweet Dream" 60
"Sweet Magic" 79

T

"Tango" 34
"The Times Rose" 51
Threepenny Bit Rose 19
"Top Marks" 60
"Touch of Class" 43
"Tournament of Roses" 43
"Trumpeter" 52
"Twoadvance" 32
"Twobe" 42

W

"Wedding Day" 75
"Wezeip" 40
"White Magic" 45
"William Lobb" 30
"William's Double Yellow" 30
"Wishing" 52

Y

"Yellow Rose of Texas" 30

Z

"Zephirine Drouhin" 75